Contents

Key

* easy

** medium

*** difficult

French food

The French love cooking, and are famous for their food. French is the language used by the world's chefs, and many kitchen tools and cookery terms are known by their French name.

Around the country

Many types of food are produced in France, because it has a very varied climate. The north is cooler, and has plenty of grass for cows to graze. Milk, butter, cream and cheese are used in dishes from this area. Lots of orchards mean that apple and pear dishes are also popular. Alsace and Lorraine in the north-east are known for pastry dishes, using local butter and cheeses.

The warmer south has a hotter, drier climate. Here, olive oil is produced, and replaces butter and cream in many recipes. In Provence and Languedoc, farmers grow vegetables such as aubergines and tomatoes. In coastal areas, there is plenty of fish to cook.

France is especially famous for its wine. The Loire, Burgundy, Bordeaux and the Champagne areas produce some of the best-known varieties.

▲ *A huge variety of fruit and vegetables are sold at local markets.*

Fresh is best

French cooks prefer fresh produce. Most towns have a market where shoppers can buy fresh local fruit and vegetables, cheese, fish and charcuterie (pronounced *sharcooteree*). This is the name for cooked and smoked meats, pâtés and sausages, as well as the name of the shops that sell these.

Every town or village has a bakery. French bread goes stale quickly, so people like to buy it fresh each day. A long, thin loaf, called a baguette, is especially popular. French people serve bread with most meals, often using it to push their food onto their forks. Cake shops, called pâtisseries (pronounced *pateeseree*), sell a range of beautiful cakes.

French meals

For breakfast, the French have a hot drink, such as coffee or hot chocolate, in a large cup or bowl. They serve it with a croissant, or bread, butter and jam. They enjoy a three- or four-course meal at lunchtime, which might be a salad, a meat or fish course, cheese and then dessert. People eat a lighter meal in the evening.

Ingredients

olive oil

tomatoes

shallots

peppers

courgettes

onions

salad leaves

bread (baguette)

olives

apricots

Camembert

leeks

mushrooms

garlic

chèvre

rosemary

raspberries

Dijon mustard

Cheese

There are hundreds of French cheeses. Brie, from the north-east, is a creamy cheese made in large discs and sold in wedges. Camembert, from Normandy, has a stronger flavour. Both these cheeses go runny in the centre when they are ripe. Other cheeses include chèvre (goat's cheese), Roquefort and the well-named Puant de Lille – stinker of Lille! Specialist cheese shops have a bigger selection than supermarkets.

Olives

In Provence, in the south, farmers grow olives, both to eat and to make into olive oil. Olive oil is available in all supermarkets. Use the cheaper oils for cooking and the more expensive ones for salad dressings. You can buy olives in cans or jars, or loose from the delicatessen counter.

Fruit

French farmers grow a lot of fruit. These include apricots, blackcurrants, strawberries, raspberries, redcurrants, cherries, melons, peaches, apples and pears. They are all available in greengrocers and supermarkets at certain times of the year.

Vegetables

French cooks use a wide variety of vegetables. More unusual ones include asparagus, chard, artichokes and mushrooms, including wild ones. The French also eat a lot of salad, using different leaves. Look out for endive, oak leaf lettuce or chicory at larger greengrocers and supermarkets.

Dijon mustard

This mustard is often added to French dishes at the end of the cooking time, or served with meat. It is made of mustard seeds and wine vinegar. Some Dijon mustard is smooth, some more grainy. You can buy it in most large supermarkets.

Garlic

Garlic is a vital ingredient of French cookery, especially in the south. The best garlic is from Languedoc, according to food experts! Prepared garlic is available in tubes and jars, but the flavour is not as good as fresh garlic.

Shallots

Shallots look like small onions, but they have a more delicate flavour. You can buy shallots from larger supermarkets and greengrocers.

Before you start

Kitchen rules

There are a few
basic rules you
should always
follow when
you are cooking:

- Ask an adult if
  you can use
  the kitchen.
- Some cooking processes, especially those
  involving hot water or oil, can be dangerous.
  When you see this sign, take extra care or ask
  an adult to help.
- Wash your hands before you start.
- Wear an apron to protect your clothes, and
  tie back long hair.
- Be very careful when using sharp knives.
- Never leave pan handles sticking out in case
  you knock them.
- Always wear oven gloves to lift things in and
  out of the oven.
- Wash fruit and vegetables before using them.

How long will it take?

Some of the recipes in this book are quick and
easy, and some are more difficult and take longer.
The strip across the top of the right hand page of
each recipe tells you how long it will take you to
cook each dish from start to finish. It also shows
how difficult each dish is to make: every recipe is
either * (easy), ** (medium) or *** (difficult).

Quantities and measurements

You can see how many people each recipe will serve at the top of each right hand page. Most of the recipes in this book make enough to feed two people. Where it is more sensible to make a larger amount, though, the recipe makes enough for four. You can multiply or divide the quantities if you want to cook for more or fewer people.

Ingredients for recipes can be measured in two different ways. Metric measurements use grams and millilitres. Imperial measurements use ounces and fluid ounces. This book uses metric measurements. If you want to convert these into imperial measurements, see the chart on page 44.

In the recipes you will see the following abbreviations:

tbsp = tablespoon   g = grams
tsp = teaspoon   ml = millilitres

Utensils

To cook the recipes in this book, you will need these utensils (as well as essentials such as spoons, plates and bowls):

- baking tray
- food processor or blender
- small and large frying pans (heavy-based, if possible)
- 20cm flan tin or sandwich cake tin
- grater
- heatproof bowl
- measuring jug
- chopping board
- saucepan (heavy-based, if possible), with lid
- set of scales
- sharp knife
- small screw-topped jar
- 1.8 litre shallow ovenproof dish
- palette knife

 Whenever you use kitchen knives, be very careful.

French onion soup

This soup is often served as a meal in itself in France, especially in the winter. Sometimes fatty bacon or ham is cooked until the fat melts. The onions are cooked in the fat and the meat added to the topping.

What you need

For the soup:
450g onions
2 tbsp oil
1 tbsp butter
2 vegetable stock cubes

For the topping:
75g Gruyère cheese
4 slices French bread

What you do

1 **Peel** the skin from the onions and cut them in half. Lay each half flat on a chopping board and **slice** it thinly.

2 Heat the oil and butter in a large saucepan. Add the onions, **cover** and cook over a low heat for 8 to 10 minutes, stirring occasionally.

3 Take the lid off the pan and cook the onions over a low heat until they are a light golden colour.

4 Pour 750ml hot water into the pan and bring it to the **boil**. Carefully crumble in the stock cubes and **simmer** for 5 minutes. Meanwhile, **grate** the cheese.

5 Put the French bread under the grill and toast one side. Turn the bread over and top with cheese. **Grill** until the cheese has melted and starts to go brown.

6 Get a spoonful of soup and blow on it to **cool** it down. Taste it and add a little salt and pepper if you like.

7 Spoon the soup into four bowls and carefully put a piece of bread into each, cheese side up. Serve, warning everyone that the cheese is piping hot!

Vichyssoise

This soup, (pronounced *veesheeswaaz*), was created by a French chef working at a New York hotel. In France, people might eat it hot or cold as a light evening meal. You may want to add 150ml milk if you are serving it cold, to make it less thick.

What you need

1 tbsp oil
3 leeks
3 medium potatoes
1 chicken or
    vegetable stock cube
284ml pot single
    cream (or milk, for
    a lower fat soup)

What you do

1 Trim the tops and roots off the leeks. Cut the leeks in half lengthways. Rinse soil off under running cold water.

(!) 2 Slice the leeks thinly.

3 Heat the oil in a large saucepan. Add the leeks, **cover** and cook them over a low heat for 5 to 8 minutes, stirring occasionally.

4 Meanwhile, **peel** the potatoes and cut them into 2½cm chunks. Take 2 tbsp leeks out of the pan and set them aside.

5 Add the potatoes, 450ml hot water and the stock cube to the leeks. Cover and **simmer** them over a low heat for about 15 minutes.

6 Allow to **cool** for 10 minutes. Carefully pour the soup into a blender or food processsor. (You may have to do this in batches; never fill a blender more than two-thirds full.) Put the lid on and process until smooth.

7 Pour back into saucepan, stir in half the cream and reheat. Take a spoonful of soup, blow it to cool it, taste it and add salt and pepper if you wish.

8 Spoon the soup into four bowls. Pour a little of the remaining cream in a spiral shape into each bowl. Place the set-aside leeks on top, and serve.

Tomato salad and green salad

Crudités (pronounced *crooditay*) are raw vegetables, served at the start of a meal. The French would just serve this simple salad with some French bread.

What you need

For the salad:
3 plum tomatoes or
   2 beef tomatoes or
   4 round tomatoes
1 shallot

For the dressing:
2 tbsp olive oil
1 tbsp white wine
   vinegar or lemon juice
1 tbsp fresh
   chopped chives
a little salt and pepper

Tomato salad

If you can, use fresh plum tomatoes or beef tomatoes, as their flavour is stronger.

What you do

1 Thinly **slice** the tomatoes and throw away the two end slices. Overlap the slices on two small plates.

2 **Peel** the shallot, and thinly slice it. Separate the rings and scatter them over the tomatoes.

3 Put the **dressing** ingredients into a screw-topped jar, put the lid on and shake well. Pour the dressing over the salad an hour before serving if possible, so that it flavours the tomatoes.

Green salad

The French have a wide variety of salad leaves to choose from. Market stalls in particular sell many different types of leafy greens, all with different flavours.

What you do

1 Wash the salad leaves in cold water. Pat them dry with a clean tea-towel and put them into a bowl.

What you need

For the salad:
50 to 75g salad leaves

For the dressing:
3 tbsp olive oil
1 tbsp white wine
   vinegar or lemon juice
¼ tsp ready made
   mustard (optional)

2 Put the dressing ingredients into a screw-topped jar with a little salt and pepper. Put the lid on, shake well, and pour over the salad. Using a large spoon and fork, gently toss the salad (turn the leaves over a few times) to coat them in dressing. Serve straight away.

Fish goujons with garlic mayonnaise

Goujons (pronounced *goojhon*) are finger-shaped strips of food. In France, cooks use sole, turbot or monkfish to make fish goujons, but any firm white fish is fine. If you use frozen fish, **thaw** it overnight in the fridge. Here, the goujons are served with garlic mayonnaise. If you prefer, add some lemon **zest** or herbs to the mayonnaise instead of the garlic.

What you need

150g skinned, filleted white fish

4 large slices stale white bread

1 egg

1 small clove of garlic

4 tbsp ready-made mayonnaise

3 tbsp vegetable oil

1 lemon

a few sprigs parsley

What you do

1 Cut the fish into strips about the size of your finger.

2 Cut the bread crusts off. Break the bread into small pieces and use a food processor to make breadcrumbs. Pour onto a plate.

3 **Beat** the egg with a fork in a bowl.

4 Dip a strip of fish into the egg until it is coated. Let any extra egg drip off. Cover the fish with breadcrumbs. Lift the fish out and put it onto a plate. Do this with all the goujons.

5 **Peel** and finely chop or crush the garlic. Put it into a small bowl and stir in the mayonnaise.

6 Heat the oil in a large frying pan over a medium heat. Add the fish goujons and **fry** until golden.

7 Using a fish slice, carefully turn the goujons over and cook the other side.

8 Cut the lemon into six long wedges.

9 Arrange the fish goujons on two plates and **garnish** with lemon and parsley. Serve with the garlic mayonnaise.

Quiche Lorraine

This egg and bacon tart, or quiche, is a speciality of the Lorraine region in north-east France. If you use a ready-made pastry case, **preheat** the oven to 180°C/350°F/gas mark 4, then go straight to step 6.

What you need

300g ready-made shortcrust pastry OR 20cm ready-made pastry case

For the filling:
100g smoked back bacon, with the rind taken off
200ml single cream
1 egg
1 egg yolk

What you do

1 Preheat the oven to 200°C/400°F/gas mark 6. Put a baking tray in the oven.

2 Sprinkle flour over a clean work surface. Roll a rolling pin over the pastry, pushing it away from you, then pulling it back. Turn the pastry a little, then roll it again. Repeat until the pastry is about 30cm wide.

3 Carefully lay it over a 20cm round flan or cake tin, easing it in. Roll the rolling pin over it to trim off the extra pastry.

4 Prick the pastry case with a fork and **chill** it for 10 minutes.

5 Put a 30cm square of non-stick baking paper into the pastry case. Fill it with any large, dried beans. Lift the tin onto the hot baking tray and put it into the oven. **Bake** the pastry for 10 minutes.

6 Meanwhile, **grill** the bacon until it is cooked. Let it cool, then cut it into small pieces.

7 To separate the egg yolk from the white, crack the egg open carefully. Keep the yolk in one half of the shell and let the white drip into a bowl. Pass the yolk between the halves until the white has all dripped out. **Beat** the yolk and the other egg together and stir in the cream.

8 (Miss this step out if using a ready-made pastry case.) Lift the pastry case out of the oven and take out the beans and paper. Turn the oven down to 180°C/350°F/gas mark 4.

9 Sprinkle the bacon into the pastry case, pour in the egg mixture and cook in the oven for 30 minutes, until the filling is set. Serve hot or cold, with salad.

Pissaladière

Pissaladière (pronounced *peessaladyair*) is a speciality of Provence, in the south of France. It is often served as a starter or light lunch. This method uses a food processor to make the base, but you could use a ready-made pizza base instead.

What you need

For the dough base:
300g strong plain flour
7g sachet easy-bake yeast
2 tbsp olive oil

For the topping:
3 tbsp olive oil
3 large onions
1 tbsp fresh rosemary
   or thyme
60g pitted black olives

What you do

1 To make the dough base, put the flour, yeast, oil and 175ml warm water into a food processor. Put the lid on and process for 3 minutes.

2 Put the dough into a bowl, cover it with a clean tea towel and leave it in a warm place for an hour. Put the dough back into the processor. Process for 2 minutes.

3 Sprinkle some flour onto a clean surface and roll the dough into a rectangle about 20cm by 30cm. Lift it onto a baking tray, place a clean tea towel over it and leave it to rise somewhere warm for 40 minutes.

4 Meanwhile **peel** and **slice** onions. Heat the oil in a large saucepan and add the onions. **Cover** and cook over a low heat for 20 minutes.

5 **Preheat** the oven to 210°C/425°F/gas mark 7.

6 Pull the green leaves from the stem of the rosemary or thyme and **chop** them finely.

7 Add the herb to the onions, stir and cook for 2 minutes. Spoon the onions over the dough base.

8 **Bake** on the top shelf of the oven for 15 minutes, then on the middle shelf for 10 to 15 minutes.

9 Scatter olives over the top and serve hot with salad.

Niçoise salad

Niçoise (pronounced *neeswaaz*) salad takes its name from Nice, in the south of France. It contains olives and tomatoes, popular ingredients in many dishes around the Mediterranean Sea. You can add a few **anchovies** if you like them.

What you need

For the salad:
4 eggs
75g French green beans
4 tomatoes
1 cos lettuce or
    2 little gem lettuces
50g pitted black olives
2 185g cans tuna

For the dressing:
3 tbsp olive oil
1 tbsp white
    wine vinegar
1 tbsp lemon juice
1 tsp mustard (Dijon,
    if possible)
a little salt and pepper

What you do

1 Put the eggs into a small saucepan and cover them with water. Bring the water to the **boil**, then **simmer** the eggs for 7 minutes.

2 Use a spoon to lift the eggs into a bowl of cold water. Tap the eggs to crack the shells. Keep topping up the cold water whilst the eggs **cool** for 5 minutes.

3 Trim the ends off the beans. Put the beans into a pan and cover with hot water. Bring to the boil and cook for 3 minutes.

4 **Drain** the beans and put them into cold water.

5 Cut the tomatoes into quarters. **Peel** off the eggshells and cut the eggs in half.

6 Tear the lettuce leaves into pieces. Wash them in cold water and gently pat them dry with a clean tea towel. Arrange them on a large plate.

7 Scatter tomatoes, eggs, drained beans and olives over the lettuce.

8 Drain the tuna, break it into chunks and scatter over the salad.

9 Put the **dressing** ingredients into a screw-topped jar and put the lid on. Shake well and pour over the salad just before serving.

Croque Monsieur

Croque Monsieur is a popular snack in France, made with bread, ham and cheese. If you add a fried egg on top, it is called a Croque Madame.

What you need

4 slices white bread
50g unsalted butter
2 thick slices smoked ham
50g Gruyère cheese
2 tbsp olive oil
rocket or other salad
    leaves to **garnish**

What you do

1 **Preheat** the grill to its lowest heat.

2 Spread one side of each slice of bread with half the butter. Place ham onto two of the slices.

3 **Grate** the cheese and put it on top of the ham, leaving a 1cm gap between the cheese and the edge of the bread.

4 Top each slice of bread with another slice, butter side down. Press firmly all the way round the edges.

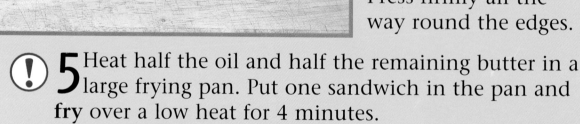

(!) **5** Heat half the oil and half the remaining butter in a large frying pan. Put one sandwich in the pan and **fry** over a low heat for 4 minutes.

6 Carefully turn the sandwich over with a fish slice. Fry for 4 minutes, until golden brown. Lift the sandwich onto a plate and put it under the grill.

7 Cook the second sandwich in the same way, following steps 5 and 6.

8 Cut both sandwiches in half, garnish with salad leaves and serve hot.

LESS FAT

Because Croque Monsieur is fried, it is very fatty. For a less fatty sandwich, heat the grill to medium, then toast one side of the sandwich until the bread has browned. Turn over and toast the other side.

25

St ak with ch rvil butter

Steak with thin chips called frites (pronounced *freet*) is a popular meal in France. The chips are sprinkled with salt and the steak is often served with herb butter and a salad. If chervil is hard to find, use parsley instead.

What you need

2 75g–100g fillet steaks
2 tbsp oil
75g mixed salad leaves

For the chervil butter:
50g butter
1 tbsp fresh chervil

For the dressing:
2 tbsp olive oil
1 tbsp lemon juice
½ tsp mustard (Dijon, if possible)
a little salt and pepper

What you do

1 Put the butter into a bowl and **mash** it with a fork. **Chop** the chervil, mix into the butter and spoon into the centre of a piece of clingfilm. Wrap it, shape it into a 3cm circle and **chill** it.

2 Place the salad into a bowl. Put the **dressing** ingredients into a screw-topped jar and put the lid on.

3 Heat the oil in a frying pan until it is very hot. Add the steak and turn the heat down to medium. **Fry** the meat for 3 minutes if you like it a bit red in the middle ('rare'), 4 minutes if you prefer it a bit pink ('medium') and 5 minutes for meat cooked right through ('well done').

4 Using a fish slice, turn the steak over and cook the other side. Lift the steak onto two plates.

5 Unwrap the butter, cut it in half and put a piece onto each steak. Shake the dressing and pour it over the salad. Toss (turn over) the salad leaves with a large spoon and fork to coat them with the dressing.

6 Serve the steak with the salad and oven chips or crusty bread.

CHERVIL

Chervil is a leafy green herb, which makes tasty herb butter. Try using parsley, chives or other herbs too. Crushed garlic in butter is also very good.

27

Gratin Dauphinois

In the Dauphiné region in the south of France, cows graze on the lower slopes of the Alps. Cheese is made from their milk and used in local dishes such as Gratin Dauphinois (pronounced *gratan dawfeenwa*). Serve it with cooked meat and salad.

What you need

6 medium potatoes
568ml pot single cream
1 clove garlic
¼ tsp ground nutmeg
50g Gruyère cheese

What you do

1 **Preheat** the oven to 180°C/350°F/gas mark 4. **Peel** and thinly **slice** the potatoes.

2 (!) Put the potatoes into a pan of hot water with a little salt. **Cover**, bring to the **boil** and **drain**. Put them into a shallow, ovenproof dish.

3 Pour the cream into a non-stick pan. Peel and crush the garlic with a fork and add it to the cream. Add the nutmeg. Gently heat the cream over a very low heat.

4 Pour the mixture over the potatoes. Cover the dish with foil and **bake** for 1 hour.

5 Finely **grate** the cheese. Take the foil off and sprinkle the cheese over the potatoes.

6 Turn the oven up to 200°C/400°F/gas mark 6 and bake for a further 15 minutes. Serve hot.

CHOOSING POTATOES

There are more than 200 different types of potato. For this recipe, choose Estima, Wilja or Maris Piper potatoes if you can find them, because they have the right texture when they are cooked. If you need to keep potatoes for a few days, put them in a cool, dark place.

Mushroom omelette

In France, omelettes are often flavoured with smoked ham, cheese or just a handful of chopped herbs, such as chives or parsley. French people use whatever they have to hand! This omelette uses little mushrooms, called button mushrooms.

What you need

50g button mushrooms
2 tbsp oil
1 tbsp butter
2 eggs
chives
chopped herbs
   to **garnish**

What you do

1 Gently wash and **slice** the mushrooms. Heat 1 tbsp of the oil in a large non-stick frying pan. Add the mushrooms and cook over a gentle heat for 3 to 4 minutes.

2 Add the butter to the pan and heat it gently. Meanwhile, break the eggs into a jug and lightly **beat** with 2 tsp cold water. Pour the egg mixture over the mushrooms, making sure that you cover the base completely.

3 Cook until the egg is starting to set (become firm) around the edges. Using a fish slice, push the mixture to the centre of the pan. Let the raw (runny) egg run to the edges and underneath the omelette, so that it all cooks.

4 Cook for a further 2 minutes or until the egg is just set. Using a fish slice, fold the omelette in half and slide it onto a plate. Garnish with chopped herbs.

VARIATIONS

Try replacing the mushrooms with **chopped** ham or chopped cooked vegetables. For a cheese omelette, add **grated** cheese just before folding the omelette in half.

Ratatouille

In Provence, in the south of France, meals are traditionally left to cook slowly during the day, while people work in the fields. This is a quicker version of a typical dish, ratatouille (pronounced *ratatooee*). It uses the vegetables that grow in the region.

What you need

1 large or
   2 medium onions
2 tbsp olive oil
2 cloves garlic
1 aubergine
2 courgettes
1 yellow pepper
1 red pepper
600g fresh tomatoes
   or 400g can chopped
   tomatoes
sprig rosemary or
   1 tsp dried rosemary

What you do

1 **Peel** and **slice** the onions. Heat the oil in a large pan, add the onions and **cover**. Cook them over a medium heat for about 5 minutes.

2 Peel and crush the garlic with a fork.

3 Cut the top and bottom off the aubergine. First, cut the aubergine into 1cm thick slices, and then into 1cm cubes.

4 Cut the top and bottom off the courgettes, and cut them in half lengthwise. Cut each half into thick slices.

5 Cut the peppers in half and throw away the seeds and the stalk. Slice each half into 2cm wide strips, and then into 2cm wide squares. If you are using fresh tomatoes, cut them into quarters.

6 Add the garlic, vegetables and rosemary to the onions, cover the pan and **simmer** over a low heat for 20 to 25 minutes

7 If you are using fresh tomatoes and rosemary, take out the tomato skins and the herb sprig.

8 Spoon the ratatouille into a serving dish. Serve with crusty bread, or with meat or fish dishes.

▲ *Ratatouille makes an ideal **vegetarian** dish.*

Apple tart

What you need

1 tbsp plain flour
500g packet flaky
  or puff pastry
4 eating apples
2 tbsp lemon juice
6 tbsp apricot jam
icing sugar to dust

Apple tarts are popular all over France, but they are a speciality in Normandy, where lots of apples grow. This version is very quick to make. If you prefer, use half the quantities to just make enough to serve 4.

What you do

1 **Preheat** the oven to 210°C/425°F/gas mark 7. **Dust** a work surface and a rolling pin with a little plain flour.

2 On the floured surface, roll the pastry with a rolling pin until it is a rectangle about 25cm by 50cm. Cut it in half crosswise to make two squares.

3 Dust two baking trays with flour and lay the pastry squares onto them. **Bake** them for 12 minutes, until they are well risen.

4 Wash the apples and take out their cores. Cut them into very thin wedges and arrange them on the pastry squares.

⚠ 5 Put the lemon juice and apricot jam in a small pan. Heat gently, until the jam has melted. Stir all the time.

6 Using a pastry brush, coat the apple slices with the lemon juice and jam **glaze**.

7 Bake the apple tarts for 5 to 8 minutes, until they are golden.

8 When they are **cool**, cut each square into four smaller squares.

9 Put a little icing sugar into a small sieve and hold it over the apple tarts. Tap the sides of the sieve to dust them with sugar.

VARIATIONS

Try using sliced strawberries, plums, apricots or raspberries to make fresh fruit tarts. If you slice them thinly, there is no need to cook the fruit before baking the tarts.

Crème brulée

Crème brulée (pronounced *crem broolay*) is a rich cream **custard** topped with hard caramel. It is a speciality around the Alps, a region famous for its dairy products. Crème brulée is a popular dessert all over France.

What you need

For the custard:
284ml pot double cream
284ml pot single cream
4 eggs
3 tbsp caster sugar
1 tbsp cornflour

For the topping:
8 tbsp soft brown sugar

What you do

1 Empty both pots of cream into a medium pan. **Beat** the eggs and the sugar together, then stir them into the cream.

2 Mix the cornflour with 2 tbsp water until it is a smooth paste. Stir it into the cream.

3 Gently cook over a very low heat, stirring all the time, until it is thick enough to coat the back of a wooden spoon. If the custard begins to form soft lumps, take the pan off the heat and beat the mixture well. Pass it through a sieve into a bowl, then carefully reheat it in a pan until it thickens.

4 Pour the custard into four small, heatproof bowls, called ramekins. Leave the custards to cool, then **chill** them overnight.

5 Sprinkle 2 tbsp soft brown sugar over each custard, making sure the sugar goes right to the edges. **Grill** until the sugar has melted and browned.

6 When they are **cool**, put the custards back in the fridge.

7 Crack the caramel top to show the custard and serve the same day.

▲ *Try serving crème brulée with fresh fruit.*

Profiteroles

Small pastry buns called profiteroles (pronounced *profeeteroll*) are used to make a special French wedding cake called a croquembouche. It is a mountain of profiteroles up to a metre high, stuck together with **caramel**.

What you need

For the pastry:
50g butter
60g plain flour
2 eggs

For the filling:
284ml pot double cream

For the sauce:
125g plain chocolate

What you do

1 **Preheat** the oven to 190°C/375°F/gas mark 5.

2 Put 150ml boiling water and the butter into a non-stick saucepan. **Cover** and heat until the butter has melted.

3 Take the pan off the heat and stir in the flour. **Beat** well with a wooden spoon to make a smooth dough.

4 Beat the eggs, and then beat a quarter of them into the dough. Continue adding all the egg mixture, a quarter at a time, beating well.

5 Scoop up a heaped teaspoon of the dough, then push it onto a baking tray using another teaspoon. Repeat this to make 20 dough balls, leaving an 8cm gap between each one.

6 **Bake** the profiteroles for 15 to 20 minutes. Lift them onto a wire rack and prick with a knife to let any steam out.

7 In a bowl, **whisk** the cream until it forms soft peaks. **Chill** it for 10 minutes.

8 Cut each profiterole in half, spoon in some cream and sandwich the halves together. Pile them onto a plate.

9 Put the chocolate in a heatproof bowl. Put it in a microwave on medium power for 1 minute, until it has melted.

10 **Drizzle** the melted chocolate over the profiteroles from a spoon. Serve the same day.

Tuiles biscuits

Formal French meals often end with coffee and a selection of marzipan sweets, chocolates or little biscuits such as these tuiles (pronounced *tweel*).

What you need

90g butter
2 egg whites
90g icing sugar
50g plain flour
100g toasted
    chopped hazelnuts
½ tsp vanilla essence
icing sugar to **dust**

What you do

1 **Preheat** the oven to 200°C/400°F/gas mark 6.

2 Melt the butter in a small pan and leave it to **cool**.

3 Put sheets of non-stick baking paper onto two baking trays.

4 Separate the egg whites from the yolks by carefully cracking open an egg. Keep the yolk in one half of the shell and let the white drip into a bowl. Pass the yolk between the halves until the white has all dripped out. Do this for both eggs.

5 Put the icing sugar, egg whites, flour, hazelnuts and vanilla essence into a bowl. **Beat** in the butter.

6 Put teaspoonfuls of the mixture onto the baking paper, pressing them flat. Leave a gap of 5cm between each one.

7 **Bake** one tray at a time for 8 to 10 minutes, until the edges are browning and the centre is set.

8 Lift the hot biscuits off the baking tray using a palette knife and lay them over a rolling pin so that they form a curved shape as they cool. Repeat to make 20 biscuits.

9 You can store tuiles in an airtight container for up to a week. Serve them dusted with icing sugar.

▲ *Tuiles might be served with coffee, ice cream or fresh fruit salad.*

Chocolate truffles

Truffles are traditionally served at the end of a special meal in France. To make them, use a continental chocolate with at least 70% cocoa solids, because this has the best flavour.

What you need

142 ml pot
    double cream
140g plain chocolate
50g white chocolate
2 tbsp cocoa

What you do

1 Put the cream into a small, non-stick saucepan. Break the plain chocolate into small pieces and add it to the cream.

2 Heat the mixture very slowly, stirring occasionally, until the chocolate has melted. Be careful not to **boil** it.

3 Take the pan off the heat, stir the mixture well and leave to **cool. Chill** for 3 hours.

4 Finely **grate** the white chocolate onto a plate. Put the cocoa onto another plate.

5 Rinse your hands under really cold water so that the mixture does not melt and stick to them!

6 Scoop out a heaped teaspoonful of the chilled truffle mixture. Quickly roll it between the palms of your hands to form a ball.

7 Put it into the white chocolate and use a fork to push it around until the truffle is well coated. Lift it onto a plate.

8 Repeat step 7 for half the truffles. If your hands are getting sticky and warm, run them under cold water again.

9 Roll the other half of the mixture in cocoa powder.

10 To serve, arrange the truffles in a small dish.

VARIATIONS

You could try coating the truffle mixture with chopped nuts instead of white chocolate and cocoa.

Further information

Here are some places to find out more about France and French cooking.

Books

Food and Festivals: France
Theresa Fisher, Hodder, Wayland, 1998.
A Little French Cookbook
Janet Laurence, The Appletree Press, 1989.
Look And Cook French Country Cooking
Ann Willan, Dorling Kindersley Ltd, 1995.
Next Stop, France
Fred Martin, Heinemann Library, 1998.

Websites

http://cooking-french.com

Conversion chart

Ingredients for recipes can be measured in two different ways. Metric measurements use grams and millilitres. Imperial measurements use ounces and fluid ounces. This book uses metric measurements. The chart here shows you how to convert measurements from metric to imperial.

SOLIDS		LIQUIDS	
METRIC	IMPERIAL	METRIC	IMPERIAL
10g	¼ oz	30ml	1 fl oz
15g	½ oz	50ml	2 fl oz
25g	1 oz	75ml	2½ fl oz
50g	1¾ oz	100ml	3½ fl oz
75g	2¾ oz	125ml	4 fl oz
100g	3½ oz	150ml	5 fl oz
150g	5 oz	300ml	10 fl oz
250g	9 oz	600ml	20 fl oz
450g	16 oz	1 litre	30½ fl oz

Healthy eating

This diagram shows you which foods you should eat to stay healthy. Most of your food should come from the bottom of the pyramid. Eat some of the foods from the middle every day. Only eat a little of the foods from the top.

Healthy eating, French style

The French love fresh fruit and vegetables, as many of the recipes in this book show. For special meals, however, some do use a lot of butter, cream and cheese. It is healthier not to eat these dishes too often!

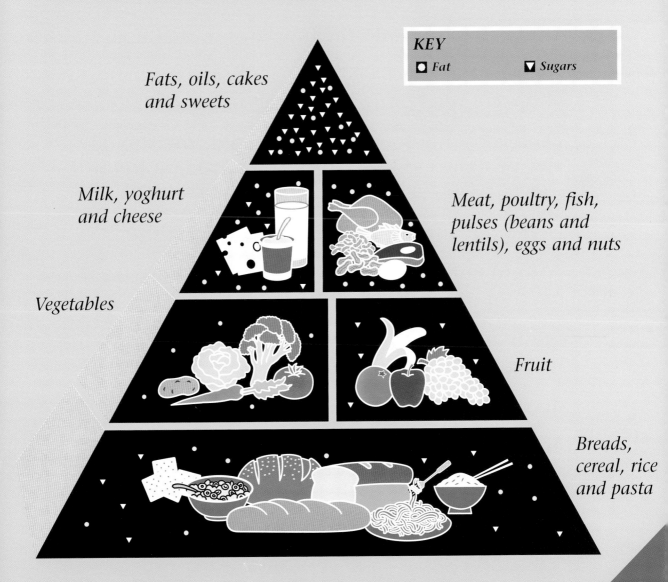

KEY
◻ *Fat*   ▽ *Sugars*

Fats, oils, cakes and sweets

Milk, yoghurt and cheese

Meat, poultry, fish, pulses (beans and lentils), eggs and nuts

Vegetables

Fruit

Breads, cereal, rice and pasta

Glossary

anchovies very small salted fish

bake cook something in the oven

beat mix something together strongly, using a fork, spoon or whisk

boil cook a liquid on the hob. Boiling liquid bubbles and steams strongly.

caramel sugar or syrup that has been heated until it turns brown. It is used to flavour or colour food.

chill put a dish into the fridge for several hours before serving

chop cut something into pieces using a knife

cool allow hot food to become cold. You should always allow food to cool before putting it in the fridge.

cover put a lid on a pan, or foil over a dish

custard milk cooked with egg to thicken it. It can be sweet or savoury.

drain remove liquid, usually by pouring something into a colander or sieve

dressing oil and vinegar sauce for salad

drizzle pour something very slowly and evenly

dust sprinkle something, such as icing sugar, lightly over food

fry cook something in oil in a pan

garnish decorate food, for example, with fresh herbs or lemon wedges

glaze coat food with something such as apricot jam to make it look glossy

grate break something, for example cheese, into small pieces using a grater

grill cook something under a grill

mash crush something, for example potatoes, until soft and pulpy

peel remove the skin of a fruit or vegetable

preheat turn on the oven in advance, so that it is hot when you are ready to put food into it

simmer cook a liquid on the hob. Simmering liquid bubbles and steams gently.

slice cut something into thin, flat pieces

thaw defrost something that has been frozen

vegetarian food which does not include meat. People who don't eat meat are called vegetarians.

whisk mix ingredients using a whisk

zest orange or lemon peel, often used finely grated

Index

Titles in the *World of Recipes* series include:

Hardback   0 431 11714 4

Hardback   0 431 11717 9

Hardback   0 431 11715 2

Hardback   0 431 11716 0

Find out about the other titles in this series on our website www.heinemann.co.uk/library